GUIDE TO
RUSSIA

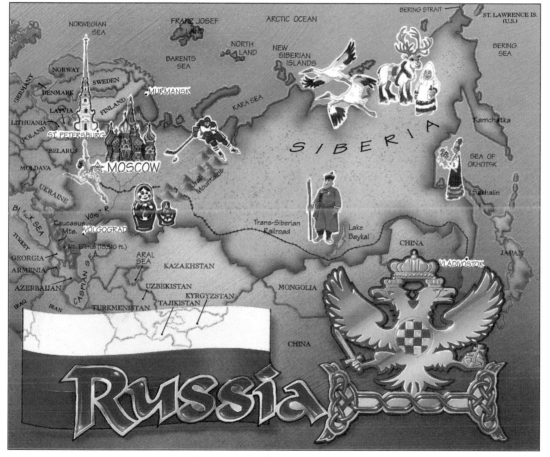

MIKE MARCH

Highlights for Children

CONTENTS

On the cover: St. Basil's Cathedral (in the center of the photograph) and the Kremlin (behind it and to the left) in Moscow, capital city of Russia

Published by Highlights for Children
© 1996 Highlights for Children, Inc.
P.O. Box 18201
Columbus, Ohio 43218-0201

10 9 8 7 6 5 4 3 2 1
ISBN 0-87534-928-5

Russia

EUROPE

ASIA

AFRICA

AUSTRALIA

ANTARCTICA

△ **The Russian flag**
Tsar Peter the Great designed Russia's flag 300 years ago. He based its design on the flag of the Netherlands, but rearranged the red, white, and blue bands. The Communists, who governed Russia (and other parts of the Soviet Union) from 1917 to 1991, used a red flag with a gold hammer and sickle. Now Peter the Great's flag is once again the national flag.

RUSSIA AT A GLANCE

Area 6,592,850 square miles (17,075,400 square kilometers)

Population 149,740,000

Capital Moscow, population 8,970,000

Other big cities St. Petersburg (5,020,000), Nizhny Novgorod (1,480,000), Novosibirsk (1,460,000)

Highest mountain Mt. El'brus, 18,510 feet (5,642 meters)

Longest river Yenisey, 2,543 miles (4,069 kilometers)

Largest lake Lake Baikal, 12,200 square miles (31,500 square kilometers)

Official language Russian

▽ **Russian postage stamps** Some stamps show buildings of Moscow's Kremlin. Sculpture and cartoon-style drawings appear on others.

▽ **Russian money** Russian currency is the *ruble*. The banknotes shown here feature the house of government at the Kremlin.

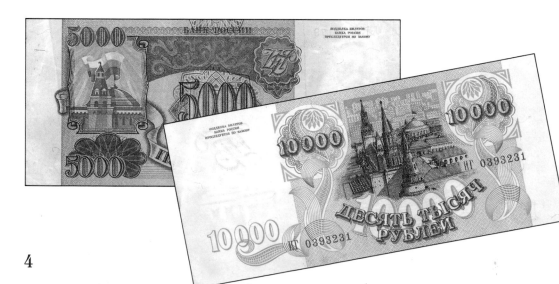

Abbreviations

Arm.	=	Armenia
Azer.	=	Azerbaijan
Est.	=	Estonia
Lat.	=	Latvia
Lith.	=	Lithuania

Greenland
(Denmark) 80°

North
Pole

Alaska (U.S.A.)
Bering Strait
170°W

ARCTIC OCEAN

Franz Josef
Land

Severnaya
Zemlya
(North Land)

Novosibirskiye Ostrova
(New Siberian Islands)

East
Siberian
Sea

180°

Barents
Sea

Novaya Zemlya

Laptev
Sea

170°E

Bering Sea

Murmansk

160°E

Kamchatka

Arkhangel'sk

Central

Verkhoyanskiy Range

Magadan

Sea of
Okhotsk

Petropavlovsk
Kamchatskiy

50°N

Siberian

Lena

Yakutsk

Perm'

West

Plain

Sakhalin

150°E

Siberian

Ob'

Yekaterinburg

Plain

Chelyabinsk

Yenisey

Omsk

Krasnoyarsk

Novosibirsk

Irtysh

Lake Baykal

Irkutsk

Vladivostok

Sea of Japan

40°N

KAZAKHSTAN

MONGOLIA

120°E

NORTH
KOREA

130°E

JAPAN

KYRGYZSTAN

TAJIKISTAN

CHINA

70°E

PAKISTAN

INDIA

80°E

90°E

100°E

© Oxford Cartographers

	RUSSIA
Ice	
Tundra	
Mountains	★ Capital
Forest	● Major Cities
Farmland	▲ Mountain Peaks
	— Country Boundaries

0   200   400 Miles

0   200   400   600   800 Kilometers

5

LAND OF FOREST AND STEPPE

Russia is the world's biggest country. It reaches nearly halfway around Earth, from the Baltic Sea in the west to the Pacific Ocean in the east. For sixty years Russia was the center of an even larger country — the U.S.S.R., or Soviet Union. Until recently, some countries that are now Russia's neighbors were part of the old Soviet Union.

Russia lies in two continents, Europe and Asia. Much of its terrain is flat and covered in the type of evergreen forest that ecologists call *taiga*. Farther south, the great prairies of the Russian *steppe* begin. The Urals, a chain of low mountains, divide Russia into two parts. Most of the country's 150 million people live in the European part, to the west of the Urals. Asiatic Russia, to the east, is a vast, beautiful wilderness called Siberia.

Russian winters are freezing cold, with lots of snow. Northeastern Siberia crosses the Arctic Circle and is one of the coldest places on Earth. But summer can bring warm sunshine to the southern parts of the country, especially to the Black Sea coast.

The Russians are a proud people with a long history. They are mostly Slavs, like other people in Eastern Europe, but they are made up of a hundred different nationalities. The Russian language is written using the Cyrillic, not Roman, alphabet.

You can visit Russia's ancient cities and explore its natural wonders by train. But the distances are so enormous that you may prefer to save time by flying. Aeroflot, one of Russia's national airlines, offers flights all over the country.

◁ **Russian folk dancers** Colorful costumes, fast music, and acrobatic leaps are all part of the rich tradition of Russian folk dancing.

▷ **Nevsky Prospekt Street, St. Petersburg** Here the sun is shining, but for much of the year this great city lies under clouds and snow.

▽ **The taiga, East Siberia** The huge pine forest that spreads across northern Russia makes up a quarter of all the world's forests.

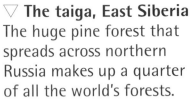

THE HISTORIC CAPITAL

The heart of Russia is its capital, Moscow. It is Russia's biggest city with nearly nine million people. Moscow lies in the west of Russia and is built on seven hills.

In the center of the city, on the north side of the Moscow River, is a huge square. This is the famous Red Square. On the east side of the square you can see the walls of the Kremlin. *Kremlin* comes from a Russian word meaning "citadel" (fortress). For many hundreds of years Russia was ruled from here. Today, the country's president has his office in the Kremlin.

Also in Red Square you will find the beautiful St. Basil's Cathedral. At night, its colorful towers and onion domes are lit up.

▷ **GUM, the largest department store in Moscow** The beautiful glass-roofed shopping center stands three stories high.

St. Basil's was built more than four hundred years ago on the orders of Tsar (sometimes spelled *czar* or *tzar*) Ivan IV. Tsars were Russian emperors. Ivan was known as "the Terrible" because he was so fierce.

The marble red building next to the Kremlin wall is the tomb of Lenin. In 1917, Vladimir Ilich Lenin led the revolution that turned Russia into a communist country. The Communists brought industry and farming under government control and banned most private business. Communism as a state party ended in Russia in 1991.

Opposite Red Square is the famous department store called GUM. Here you can buy traditional Russian souvenirs, such as a *balalaika* (a stringed instrument) or a set of *matreshka* dolls. Matreshka dolls pull apart and fit inside one another.

Getting around in Moscow is fun. The subway trains are fast, and the stations are beautifully decorated. Go to a traditional restaurant to try popular Russian dishes such as *borscht* (beet soup) or the expensive delicacy, *caviar* (salted eggs of sturgeons, a type of fish). For an evening show, be sure to visit the Bolshoi Ballet or the Moscow State Circus. Both are world famous.

◁ **The Moscow River and the Kremlin** The golden onion domes of the Kremlin's churches rise above the fortress walls. An onion dome is a type of roof on Russian churches.

▽ **Clowns of the Moscow State Circus** The world-famous circus has more than 6,000 performers.

HEROES, TSARS, AND COMMUNISTS

You can walk right around the Kremlin on the top of its red brick wall. The distance is 1.4 miles (2.25 kilometers). By Trinity Tower the wall rises to 65 feet (20 meters) high, and in places it is 20 feet (6 meters) wide. The Russian Yuri Gagarin is one of the Russian heroes who are buried with honor in the Kremlin wall. Gagarin was the world's first *cosmonaut* (Russian name for astronaut). He was killed in a plane crash in 1968.

The Kremlin began as a wooden fort, built by a Russian prince nearly 850 years ago. It is the oldest part of Moscow. But the old wooden buildings were burned down during wars. The great cathedrals that now stand in the Kremlin date from the 1490s. The tsars were crowned here. They lived in the Great Kremlin Palace, which was rebuilt in the 1800s. Today the Russian parliament meets in the Kremlin.

Walk across Red Square to explore Moscow's old merchant quarter. Here you will find a street lined with beautiful old churches and stone houses from the time of Ivan the Terrible. Behind the Kremlin, on the western side, you can stroll down the famous Arbat cobblestone street and mingle with crowds of shoppers to the sounds of lively street musicians.

Near the old city wall stands the gray-and-brown Lubyanka building. This was once a prison. It was also the headquarters of the communist secret police, the KGB.

Gorky Park, on the south bank of the Moscow River, is a fine place to relax. Here, in summer, you can take a boat ride on a lake and watch the black swans. In winter the park becomes a giant ice-skating rink.

◁ **The Tsar Bell** The world's biggest bell stands in Moscow's Kremlin. It weighs 200 tons. The bell was cast in the 1730s, but it broke during a fire in 1737.

◁ **The Kremlin, Moscow** The Bell Tower of Ivan the Great, on the left, stands 263 feet (80 meters) high. Next to it is the Cathedral of St. Michael the Archangel.

▽ **Street traders in Moscow's Lenin Hills district** On sale are *matreshka* dolls and video and audio tape cassettes. Since the end of Communism, street markets have appeared all over Moscow. Everything from apples to old army uniforms is sold.

CULTURE AND RELIGION

Northwest of Moscow lies a little town called Klin. Peter Ilich Tchaikovsky, Russia's most famous composer, spent his later years here. The large house where Tchaikovsky lived is now a museum where his piano is on display. Tchaikovsky wrote the ballet *Swan Lake*. His music is popular all over the world.

If you follow the road from Klin, you come to Tver'. This is an ancient city, which 500 years ago was as powerful as Moscow. Europe's longest river, the Volga, runs through Tver'. The Volga begins its journey farther west, in a lovely upland region of lakes and pine forests. In summer, people come here to fish and to go hiking or canoeing.

Northeast of Moscow there is a group of beautiful old towns known as the Golden Ring. Nearest to the capital is Sergiyev Posad. The town is named after the Trinity St. Sergius Monastery, which has stood here since 1340. The main church is made of white stone and has huge blue onion domes studded with golden stars. The monastery is one of the oldest centers of the Russian Orthodox Church. Russians are traditionally Christians whose form of worship is called Orthodoxy. Orthodox Christianity came to Russia long ago from Byzantium, which is now Turkey.

The Communists did not agree with religion. They closed many churches and turned others into museums. They even renamed the town of Sergiyev Posad as Zagorsk after V. M. Zagorsky, a senior Communist Party official.

Nizhny Novgorod, on the Volga River, is another old town. Today it is Russia's third-largest city. Nearby, you can visit a factory where matreshka dolls are made.

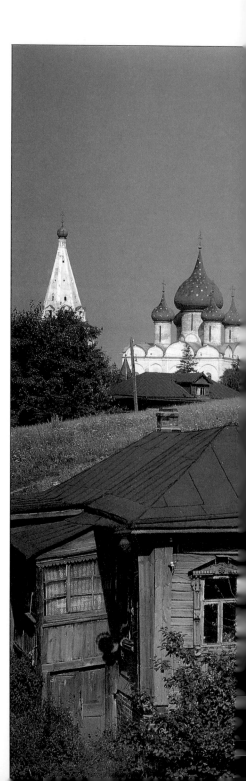

▷ **Suzdal', an ancient town in the Golden Ring**
Many of the houses are wooden. The churches are made of wood, white stone, or brick.

12

▷ **A Russian boy with his grandmother** *Babushka*, a word for grandmother, also means a type of headscarf.

▽ **Shopping the Russian way** Sugar, canned foods, candy, and even cola are on sale. Today's stores are even more modern.

THE WESTERN FRONTIER

Traditionally, Russians made tea using a *samovar*, a metal urn in which the water boils over hot coals. The home of the samovar is Tula, an industrial town south of Moscow. Samovars have been made here for more than two hundred years. But Tula is also famous for its gunsmiths. Their work is shown in a museum here, from the earliest musket to the modern Kalashnikov rifle.

Wild boars and brown bears live in the vast forests around the town of Bryansk. The region lies on Russia's borders with Ukraine and Belarus. These two countries, like others to the west and south of Russia, were once states of the Soviet Union. From Bryansk, you can take a trip to Dyat'kovo to watch glassblowers and glasscutters at work in the town's famous factory.

Smolensk is an ancient border town farther north on the steep banks of the Dnepr River. For six years, between 1596 and 1602, 30,000 people worked from dawn until dusk to build the great city walls of Smolensk. Even today, in spite of damage by countless invading armies, the walls are an impressive sight.

◁ **A beautiful wooden chalet** It is painted in bright colors and decorated with storybook carvings. In many Russian villages, it is the custom for local carpenters and painters to each contribute part of the decorations of such houses.

▷ **A Russian chef** He has prepared *shashlyk* — chunks of lamb grilled on a skewer, often served in a spicy tomato sauce. The dish comes from the Caucasus region, in southern Russia, but is popular throughout the country.

The magnificent city of Pskov has a thousand-year history. Outside the city is a museum that was once the Pushkin family estate. Alexander Pushkin, Russia's greatest poet, is buried here in a monastery on the wooded hills named after him.

Pskov has been called "Novgorod's little brother." The name "Novgorod" means "new town," but Novgorod is one of Russia's oldest cities. The first records of Russian history were kept here. They were written on the bark of birch trees. Perhaps that is why the birch is Russia's national tree.

"Window on Europe"

In 1712, Tsar Peter the Great moved the capital north from Moscow to a new city on the edge of the Baltic Sea. Built on marshy ground at the mouth of the Neva River, it was to be Russia's "window on Europe." Peter called the city St. Petersburg, after himself. The new Russian navy was launched from here.

St. Petersburg is now Russia's second-largest city, with more than five million people. The fine buildings, broad avenues, and many waterways make St. Petersburg one of the world's most beautiful cities.

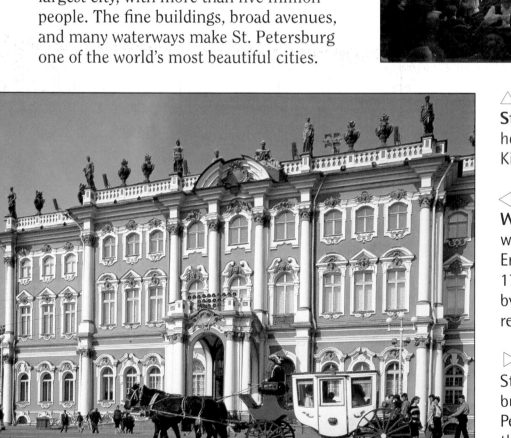

△ **Mariinsky Theater, St. Petersburg** This is the home of the world–famous Kirov, or Mariinsky, Ballet.

◁ **A coach ride by the Winter Palace** The palace was built for the Russian Empress Elizabeth in the 1700s. It was badly damaged by fire in 1837, but was soon restored to its former glory.

▷ **Peter and Paul Fortress** St. Petersburg's oldest building is on Hare Island. Peter the Great is buried in the cathedral with the tall spire in the center.

In winter, the waterways and even the rivers freeze over, and people use them as roads. Because St. Petersburg lies so far north, it has very few daylight hours in winter. But in summer, for the last weeks of June, the sun never sets here. You can join in the *White Nights* festival at the ballet or an open-air concert. Or you could take an all-night sea cruise.

For more than 150 years, Russia's rulers lived in the great Winter Palace on the south bank of the Neva River. Then, in spring 1917, Tsar Nicholas II gave up the throne. Nine months later Lenin and his supporters seized power. They stormed the Winter Palace at a signal shot fired from the river by the battle cruiser *Aurora*. The old ship now lies at anchor here as a museum. Once Lenin was in control, he moved the capital back to Moscow. From 1924 to 1991 St. Petersburg was known as Leningrad.

The Winter Palace is the largest of the old royal buildings that are now part of the State Hermitage Museum. This is one of the world's greatest collections of art treasures, from earliest times to the present.

GOING NORTH

Some Russians who live in cities have a small summer cottage in the country to use during vacations. This type of home is called a *dacha* and is usually made of wood. You can see plenty of dachas north of St. Petersburg.

Farther north is the Karelia region, which shares a long border with Finland. In fact, Karelia once belonged to Finland, and some people here have Finnish ancestors.

Karelia is mostly flat and covered in beautiful forests and lakes. The region's main town is Petrazavodsk. It stands on the shores of Lake Onega, one of the biggest lakes in Europe. From here you can take a hydrofoil out to the old monastery on Kizhi Island. As you approach the island, the cluster of onion domes coming into view is an amazing sight. They belong to two magnificent wooden cathedrals. The larger of these has twenty-two domes grouped close together to look like a huge fir tree. It was built in 1703 without the use of nails.

Karelia stretches as far north as the Arctic Circle. Beyond here are the Kola Peninsula and the big port city of Murmansk. The winters bring nearly two months of nonstop darkness to the town. But it is not as cold as it sounds, because of the Gulf Stream. This warm ocean current keeps Murmansk harbor from freezing. Around Murmansk there are smelting works for nickel, which is mined in the region.

You can cross the White Sea from the Kola Peninsula to the port of Arkhangel'sk. Most of the timber that Russia sells abroad leaves from here. To the south, the Vologda region is famous for its lacemaking and its delicious butter. This is churned using a secret recipe that includes nuts.

▷ **Vyborg Castle** Vyborg is a Russian town on the Gulf of Finland. The oldest parts of the castle were built by the Swedes in 1293.

18

▷ **Solovetsky Monastery** In the 1400s Russian monks built the monastery on islands in the White Sea. The massive stone walls of the monastery's kremlin were added about a hundred years later.

▽ **Modern Engels Street in Arkhangel'sk** The city was founded by Ivan the Terrible in 1584.

THE CAUCASUS

Sochi is a popular vacation resort on the Black Sea coast. A mild climate, brightly colored spring flowers, good beaches, and hot springs draw thousands of visitors here every year. Regular flights to Sochi leave from Moscow and St. Petersburg, as well as other cities. The town lies in the foothills of the beautiful Caucasus Mountains. These protect the Black Sea coast from the harsh winter winds blowing from the north.

Sochi is a beautiful town with many trees and shrubs, but it is very busy. To get away from the crowds, you can visit a tea farm set in wooded hills and taste a brew made from local leaves. Farther inland, in Central Caucasus, there are mineral water springs scattered among volcanoes that no longer erupt. Towns such as Pyatigorsk have grown up around the springs and have been popular as health resorts for many years.

◁ **People relaxing on the beach at Dagomys** The Black Sea resort of Dagomys, 12 miles (19 kilometers) north of Sochi, lies among wooded hills and lush green vegetation. Dagomys is also a major tea plantation center.

▷ **A scene in the Caucasus** An old defensive wall stands on a stony riverbank overlooked by rugged hills. The Caucasus Mountains reach from the Black Sea to the Caspian Sea. The mountains' lower slopes are covered with oak, chestnut, and Caucasian fir trees.

From Pyatigorsk, go south into the Caucasus Mountains to explore the great Mt. El'brus, the highest mountain in Europe. It is 18,510 feet (5,609 meters) tall. You can take a cable car more than halfway to the top. The view from where the cable car stops is breathtaking.

In the mountains you can follow the hiking trails that lead to spectacular gorges, roaring waterfalls, blue lakes, and ancient glaciers. You can visit a nature park where bison, deer, bears, tuft-eared lynxes, and the black griffon bird all have their homes.

The Dagestan region, in the eastern Caucasus, is famous for its finely woven carpets. Many people here live in hillside villages. They are mostly Muslims, followers of the religion Islam. Since the 1100s, the people have held a Sunday carpet market in Derbent, a town on the Caspian coast.

▽ **A sturgeon caught in the Volga Delta** Sturgeon of the Black Sea grow to 16 feet (5 meters) in length.

21

THE VOLGA AND THE DON

The road and railroad from the Caucasus to Moscow pass through Rostov na Donu. This is a big industrial city and a major port. It lies on the Don River, not far from where the Don flows into the Azov Sea. The city is surrounded by cornfields and fields of grapes for making into wine and Russian champagne.

In the 1400-1500s, bands of people settled on the banks of the Don. Many of them had run away from life as serfs (slave-like peasant farmers). They were called Cossacks. Later they defended Russia's borders. They were fierce warriors who were famous for their horseriding skills.

If you take a steamboat upriver, you pass the old Don Cossack capital, which is now a peaceful village. Here you can visit ancient Cossack houses built like forts and the church where the *ataman*, or Cossack leader, used to pray.

The Don River joins the slow-flowing Volga River at the Volga-Don Canal. To move between the two rivers, ships pass through thirteen locks. Thanks to Russia's canals, big ships can sail all the way from the Arctic to the Black Sea.

One of the proudest cities on the Volga is Volgograd, which was formerly called Stalingrad. A huge statue of the Motherland, sword in hand, stands on a hill overlooking the city. It is a monument to the heroes who saved the city from capture during a World War II battle in 1942.

Sailing on up the Volga, you pass wooded hills, forests where deer roam, cornfields, and watermelon groves. In between are industrial towns, such as Togliatti, where Samara cars are made. You leave the ship at the ancient city of Kazan', ten days after steaming out of Rostov na Donu.

▷ **A streetcar in downtown Rostov na Donu** An onion-domed cathedral overlooks the central square of this modern city. More than a million people live here.

▽ Hydroelectric dam, near Volgograd The dam has created a huge reservoir 350 miles (560 kilometers) long on the Volga River. The largest of the Volga's dams, it produces some of the world's least expensive electricity.

△ A vegetable market in Volgograd Women from farms outside the city sell potatoes (by weight) and other vegetables to shoppers.

TRAIN TO SIBERIA

Many of the people you see in Kazan' are Tatars. Long ago, Tatar armies from Asia swept across Europe. They built a vast empire, of which Russia was part. The Tatars moved around from place to place, living in goatskin huts called *yurts*. A few Tatars still live like this on the banks of the Volga, but in permanent settlements.

From Kazan' the railroad to the east crosses a chain of rocky hills. These are the Ural Mountains, which divide Europe from Asia. Yekaterinburg, farther down the track, is one of 800 stations on the great Trans-Siberian Railroad. The line goes all the way from Moscow to Vladivostok, a port on the Pacific Coast. It is the longest railway in the world. The train travels 5,800 miles (9,300 kilometers), crossing seven time zones.

Past Yekaterinburg, the train enters the vast Siberian wilderness. You see the endless, dense, damp forest called the taiga. Pine, spruce, and fir trees stretch as far as the eye can see. Farther south are the flat, dry prairies, or steppes.

Novosibirsk, on the great Ob River, is Siberia's biggest town. It grew rapidly with the coming of the Trans-Siberian Railroad in the 1890s. Today it has the biggest railroad station in the region and the biggest opera and ballet theater in the whole country.

Farther east, Irkutsk is a modern city that began as a Siberian Cossack camp in the 1650s. It lies on the Angara River, which flows westward from Lake Baikal into the Yenisey, Russia's longest river. During the Irkutsk winter festival you can ride through the snow in a *troika*, a sleigh pulled by three horses side-by-side, and feast on *bliny* (Russian pancakes) in the forest.

▷ **The Trans-Siberian Railroad at Omsk station** Omsk lies 390 miles (630 kilometers) west of Novosibirsk. Omsk is Siberia's second-largest city.

◁ **Khanty women making clothes** The Khanty are a people who live around the Ob River in western Siberia. They used to be roving hunters, but most now live in villages.

▽ **A modern Don's Cossack and his horse** Cossacks were traditionally the horsemen of the great grasslands of the southern Russian steppes.

RUSSIA'S FAR EAST

From Irkutsk, the Trans-Siberian Railroad follows the southern shores of Lake Baikal. You get wonderful views of the lake and the surrounding mountains from the train. "The blue eye of Siberia," as Lake Baikal is known, is the oldest lake in the world. It is home to Arctic seals and to thousands of plants and fish found nowhere else.

Crossing the Amur River, the train passes close to the border with China. From the next town, Khabarovsk, you can fly north to Yakutsk. This city, on the Lena River, is the capital of a huge empty region about three times the size of Alaska. Much of it is marshy land that, deep down, is frozen all the time. This is called tundra. New buildings in Yakutsk stand on concrete stilts. Without these pillars, heat from the building turns the ground to mud and causes the building to sink.

Winters are so cold here that your breath can freeze. In winter people wrap themselves in furs to keep warm. The local people, the Yakut, have always been great hunters and trappers, and fur trading is a long tradition. So too is reindeer herding, especially among the Chuchki people.

The region is rich in minerals. Oil, gas, coal, tin, gold, and diamonds are all found here or in the Magadan region to the east. In the past, many Russian prisoners were brought here to work in the mines and build new roads.

Your journey across Russia on the Trans-Siberian Railroad finally comes to an end at the city of Vladivostok. This port on the Sea of Japan is where the Russian navy's Pacific Fleet is based. You can fly home from Vladivostok, but before you leave be sure to visit a nature park in the taiga to see the beautiful Siberian Tiger.

▷ **Listvyanka village** This small village lies on the shores of Lake Baikal, near Irkutsk. The painted wooden houses are typical of this region.

▽ **Lake Baikal** Russia's biggest lake is also the world's deepest. The water is always cold, and in winter it is covered by 30 feet (9 meters) of ice.

△ **Reindeer roundup in northern Siberia**
For centuries, the Chuchki people have roamed the tundra with their reindeer herds.

RUSSIA FACTS AND FIGURES

People

Russians come from more than a hundred different nationalities. Most are descendants of Slavs from Eastern Europe. Many are also partly of Scandinavian or Tatar origin. The Tatars are the largest group of the non-Slavic Russians. In Siberia, the Buryats and the Yakuts are the largest ethnic groups. A few Germans, Jews, and Koreans also live in Russia.

Trade and Industry

Iron ore and nickel are found in northwest Russia, around the Arctic Circle. Copper and zinc, as well as precious metals such as gold and platinum, are mined in the Urals and Siberia. Raw materials supply the needs of Russia's traditional heavy industries, such as steelmaking. They also bring in money from sales abroad.

Russia produces more gas than any other country and has huge oil fields and coal fields. Electrical power is also produced from hydroelectic dams on major rivers, such as the Volga and Yenisey.

Timber is another important natural resource.

△ **An outdoor Russian Orthodox Church service** The priests are wearing the traditional long robes and tall hats.

Fishing

The Russian fishing fleet is one of the world's biggest. It operates from the Arctic to the Pacific.

Fish caught include haddock, cod, halibut, herring, sardines, tuna, anchovy, crab, shrimp and other shellfish, squid and octopus. Beluga sturgeon is caught in the Caspian Sea and the Volga Delta.

The many rivers are fished for salmon, pike, perch, and trout.

Farming

Only about one-tenth of the land is suitable for farming, but Russia grows more potatoes than any other country. It is also the biggest producer of oats, rye, and barley. Other crops include sugar beets, apples, plums, grapes, tobacco, tea, cabbage, and other vegetables.

Many farmers raise pigs and chickens to sell at market, and cattle are raised for both meat and milk. Russia is a major producer of wool, and sheep provide meat as well.

Food

The main meal of the day is *obed* (lunch). This usually includes soup and black rye bread. Ice cream is a popular dessert. Here are a few typical Russian dishes:
solyanka: a thick soup with fish or meat and salted cucumbers
pelmeni: Siberian-style dumplings, stuffed with meat, in sour cream
khatchapuri: hot cheese bread
shchi: cabbage soup
zharkoe po domashnemu: ("homemade hotpot") chicken stewed in a clay pot and served with potatoes and mushrooms

Schools

All children must go to school between the ages of 6 and 15. They study mathematics, sciences, and other subjects, including a foreign language, which is often English. School lasts from Monday to Saturday. After 15, some children stay at school to prepare for entry to a university or college of technololgy.

The Media

The main national daily newspapers are *Pravda* (Truth) and *Izvestiya* (News), and there are many regional daily papers. Some appear in the local language rather than Russian. The many weeklies include *Moscow News*, published in English, and *Argumenty I Fakty* (Arguments and Facts), one of the world's biggest-selling newspapers.

Magazines cover everything from general news (*Ogonyok*) to new writing (*Novy Mir*), humor (*Krokodil*), and sports. *Muzzitka* is a popular children's magazine.

There are six national television and radio channels and many regional ones. Most programs are in Russian.

△ **Ballerina and partner from Moscow's Bolshoi Ballet** The ballet group is based at the Bolshoi Theater, which was founded in 1776.

Music

Russian music has its roots in folk song and the singing of the Russian Orthodox Church. From the 1800s, Russian composers used these traditions in writing operas, ballets, and other forms of music. The opera *Prince Igor* by Alexander Borodin (1833-87) and the suite *Sheherazade* by Nikolai Rimsky-Korsakov (1844-1908) are examples. But the best-loved of 19th century composers is Peter Ilich Tchaikovsky. He wrote ballets, symphonies, concertos, and much more.

Later Russian composers were Sergei Rachmaninov, Igor Stravinsky, and Sergei Prokofiev. During the Communist period, Dmitry Shostakovich (1905-75) composed a number of vast symphonies.

Art

Up to the time of Peter the Great, icons were the main art form. These were religious paintings done on wood. They showed Christ or Mary or the saints. The greatest icon painter was Andrey Rublyov (1380-1430). In the 1800s, artists such as Ilya Repin painted pictures to highlight the problems of poor people.

Later, famous Russian artists include Vassily Kandinsky, Marc Chagall, the abstract painter Kazemir Malevich, and Aleksandr Rodchenko, who invented poster design. Ivan Glazunov is an outstanding Russian artist of the present day. Russia has also produced a number of famous movie directors, especially Sergei Eisenstein and Andrey Tarkovsky.

29

RUSSIA FACTS AND FIGURES

Literature and Drama

The "father" of modern Russian literature was Alexander Pushkin. Other Russian authors have written some world-famous books and plays. They include: *Crime and Punishment* by Fyodor Dostoyevsky, *War and Peace* and *Anna Karenina* by Leo Tolstoy, the play *The Cherry Orchard* by Anton Chekhov, and *Dr. Zhivago* by Boris Pasternak. Maxim Gorky wrote about poor people. Writer Alexander Solzhenitsyn is famous for his novels attacking the ideals of Communism.

Religion

Russia has no official religion. Traditionally, Russians were Orthodox Christians. Other religions include Islam, Buddhism, and Judaism. All religion was suppressed by the Communists.

Festivals

Some old Russian holidays are:
March/April **Paskha** (Easter)
Early June **Tun-Payram** Opening of Summer Pastures
25 December for 12 days **The Russian Winter Festival** Troika rides, folk dancing, and circuses

△ **A school classroom in Samara, a city on the Volga River** Russian school children take an examination every year.

Sports

Soccer is the favorite sport among Russian spectators. Ice hockey, basketball, volleyball, weightlifting, and wrestling are also popular among spectators and participants. Horseracing attracts huge crowds. Skiing and ice-skating are very popular. In fact, Russia has won a large number of its Olympic medals for ice-skating events. Russians also like to swim, climb mountains, and go fishing.

Many people also play chess. Russian chessplayers are among the best in the world.

Plants

Pines, fir, spruce, and larch cover the taiga. Mosses, lichens, and grasses grow in the northern tundra.

Farther south, Amur lilac, ginseng, lianas, black fir, and Manchurian ash and walnut grow. Mongolian oak, hornbeam, linden, and maple trees are found near the border with China. Silver birch flourish in the highlands between the tundra and taiga. Most of the plants in the steppes are drought-resistant grasses and sedges. The slopes of the Caucasus are covered with oak, beech, chestnut, and Caucasian fir.

Animals

Seals and polar bears live on Russia's northern shores. Wolves and reindeer roam the tundra and taiga forest inland. Moose, lynx, elk, brown bears, sable, and hazel grouse have a home in the vast forests of the taiga. In summer, the tundra and the Volga Delta teem with ducks, geese, and wading birds. The Siberian tiger and rare Amur leopard live in southeast Siberia along with bears, musk deer, and more than 300 different kinds of birds.

HISTORY

People have lived in Russia for more than half a million years. Slavs from eastern Europe settled in the country about 150,000 years ago. In the 800s A.D., Vikings from Scandinavia set up the first Russian capital.

Russia was invaded by Tatar and Mongol armies from Asia in the 1200s and remained under their rule for the next 250 years. In 1480, Moscow was made the new capital by Prince Ivan III. His grandson, Ivan the Terrible, had himself crowned as Russia's first tsar (emperor). Under Tsar Peter I ("the Great"), Empress Catherine, and Tsar Alexander I, Russia expanded its borders.

In 1917, the last of Russia's tsars, Nicholas II, gave up the throne after Russia suffered bad losses in World War I. Later that year Lenin, who led the party called Bolsheviks, launched a revolution and seized power. He changed the names of the party to Communist and the country to Union of Soviet Socialist Republics (U.S.S.R., or Soviet Union). Joseph Stalin was its dictator from 1929 to 1953.

During Stalin's rule, the Soviet Union established Communist governments in the countries of Eastern Europe. This worried the United States and western European countries. A tense period known as the Cold War followed. In the late 1980s, while the famous Soviet leader Mikhail Gorbachev was president, the Communists lost control of Eastern Europe. The U.S.S.R. broke up into Russia and other independent countries. Boris Yeltsin was elected president of Russia in 1991.

LANGUAGE

Russia's official language is Russian. It is spoken all over the country. However, many of Russia's different peoples speak their own languages as well. Russian is a Slavonic language, like those of Eastern Europe. It has its own alphabet, called Cyrillic. This developed from the Greek alphabet and looks similar to it. It was St. Cyril, a Greek monk, who first gave Russia a written language in the ninth century. In spoken Russian the stress falls heavily on some syllables and not on others.

Useful words and phrases

English	Russian
Zero	nul'
One	adeen
Two	dva
Three	tree
Four	chetyre
Five	pyat'
Six	shest'
Seven	syem'
Eight	vosem'
Nine	dyevyat'
Ten	dyesyat'
Sunday	vaskresyen'e
Monday	panedyel'nik
Tuesday	vtornik

Useful words and phrases

English	Russian
Wednesday	sreda
Thursday	chetvyerg
Friday	pyatnitsa
Saturday	subbota
Hello	Zdrastvuti
Good morning	Dobroye utra
Good evening	Dobry vyecher
Good night	Spakoynoy nochi
Good-bye	Dosvidán'ya
Please	Pazhaluysta
Thank you	Spaseeba
How are you?	Kak pazhivayete?
Very well, thank you	Kharasho, spaseeba

INDEX

Acknowledgments
Book created for Highlights for Children, Inc.
by Bender Richardson White
Editors: Peter MacDonald and Lionel Bender
Designer: Malcolm Smythe
Art Editor: Ben White
Editorial Assistant: Madeleine Samuel
Picture Researcher: Annabel Ossel
Production: Kim Richardson

Maps produced by Oxford Cartographers, England.
Banknotes from Thomas Cook Currency Services.
Stamps from Stanley Gibbons.

Editorial Consultant: Andrew Gutelle
Guide to Russia has been approved by Joan Padro, Ph.D., Russian Television Consultant and Translator, London
Russia Consultant: Maria Lukashkina, Children's Publication Editor, Moscow, and Dr. Yulia Prosalkova, Dept. of International Connections, Russian State Library, Moscow
Managing Editor, Highlights New Products: Margie Hayes Richmond

Picture credits
EU = Eye Ubiquitous/David Cumming, RRPL= Russia & Republic's Photo Library/Mark Wadlow.
Z = Zefa. t = top, b = bottom, l = left, r = right.
Cover: RRPL. Pages 6, 7t: Z. 7b, 8, 9t, 9b, 10, 11t: RRPL. 11b:EU. 12-13: Z. 13t, 13b: EU. 14: Z/Steenmans. 15l: RRPL. 15r: Z. 16tr: Eye Ubiquitous/N. Wiseman. 16bl: Z/Janicek. 17,18-19: Z. 19t, 19b: RRPL. 20: EU. 21r: EU. 21l: RRPL. 22-23: RRPL. 21t, 21b: EU. 24-25:RRPL. 25t: Z. 25b: EU. 26-27: RRPL. 27t: Z/Sunak. 27b: Z. 28: EU. 29: RRPL. 30: EU. *Illustration on page 1* by Tom Powers.